ANIMALS ARE AMAZING

SNAKES

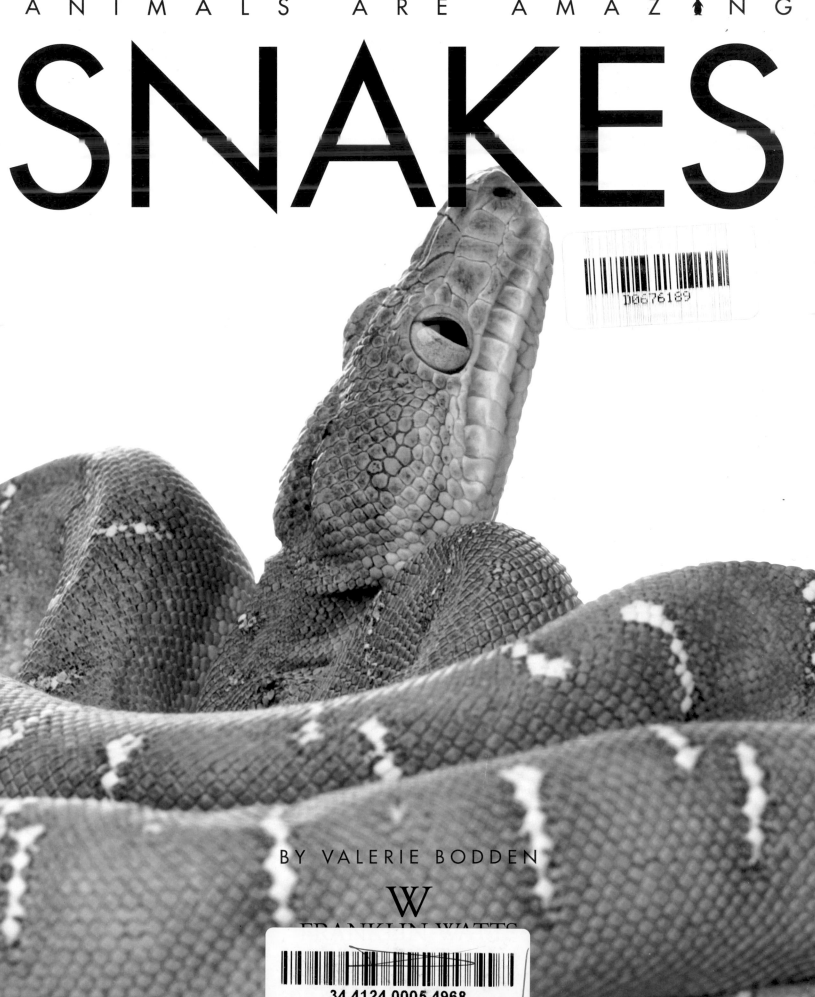

BY VALERIE BODDEN

W
FRANKLIN WATTS

This edition published in the UK in 2014 by
Franklin Watts
338 Euston Road
London NW1 3BH

Franklin Watts Australia
Level 17/207 Kent Street
Sydney NSW 2000

First published by Creative Education,
an imprint of the Creative Company.
Copyright © 2010 Creative Education
International copyright reserved in all countries.
No part of this book may be reproduced in any
form without written permission from the publisher.

ISBN: 978 1 4451 2957 0
Dewey number: 597.96'

A CIP catalogue record for this book
is available from the British Library.

Printed in China

Franklin Watts is a division of
Hachette Children's Books
an Hachette UK company
www.hachette.co.uk

Book and cover design by The Design Lab
Art direction by Rita Marshall

Photographs by Corbis (Brandon D. Cole,
Michael & Patricia Fogden), Dreamstime (Hotduckz),
Getty Images (Tom Bean, DEA PICTURE LIBRARY,
George Grall, Pete Oxford, Thad Samuels Abell Ii,
Roy Toft), iStockphoto (Eric Isselée, Mark Kostich,
Ian McDonnell), Minden Pictures (Pete Oxford)

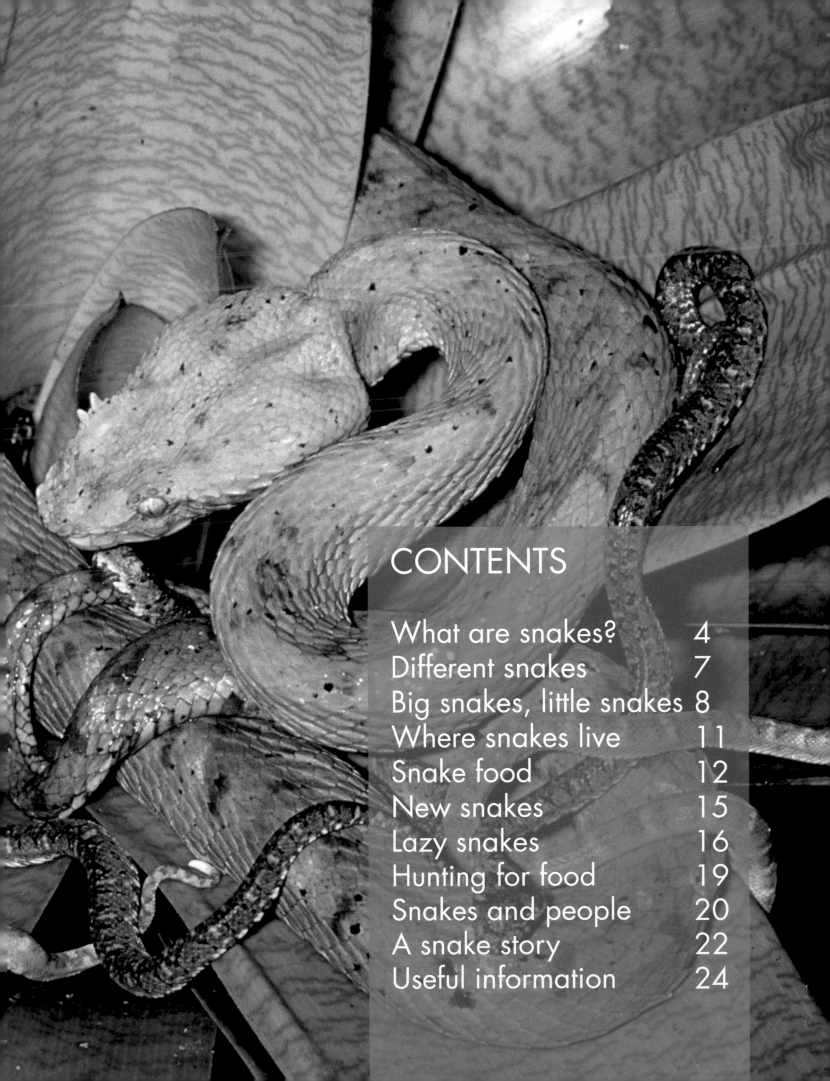

CONTENTS

What are snakes?

All snakes bend and twist their bodies to move.

Snakes are long, thin **reptiles**. They do not have any legs. There are about 2,700 types of snake in the world.

reptiles animals that have scales and a body that is always as warm or as cold as the air around it.

Different snakes

A snake uses its tongue like other animals use their noses.

Snakes are covered with **scales**. The scales help protect the snakes. Snakes come in lots of colours. Some are green, red or black. Others have spots or stripes on their bodies. Snakes have a **forked** tongue. They use their tongue to pick up smells from the air.

scales small, hard and tough plates that lie on top of the snake's skin. Scales are made from the same stuff as your fingernails.
forked split into two or more parts.

Big snakes, little snakes

A snake called a boa is one of the biggest types.

Some snakes are tiny. They can be smaller than a worm. Other snakes are huge. They can be almost as long as a bus! Some snakes are very heavy. The green **anaconda** (*an-uh-KON-duh*), a type of snake called a boa, can weigh as much as four grown people.

anaconda   a huge snake that lives in South America.

Where snakes live

Snakes live all around the world. Some snakes live in the grass. Other snakes can climb trees and live in forests. Some live in **deserts**. Some kinds of snakes even live in water. They have a special, flat tail to help them swim.

Sea snakes live and swim in the ocean, just like fish.

deserts big, dry areas where few plants can grow. They are often very hot and covered with sand.

Snake food

Snakes eat many kinds of animals. Some snakes eat frogs or mice. Others eat birds. Some really big snakes eat monkeys or deer. A snake's head can **expand** to be as wide as their **prey**. They swallow the animals whole!

This snake is swallowing a big rat for dinner!

expand to stretch really wide or spread out.
prey animals that are eaten by other animals.

New snakes

Most mother snakes lay eggs. Baby snakes **hatch** out of the eggs. Other snakes give birth to live babies. Mother snakes do not take care of the baby snakes. As the baby snakes grow, they **shed** their old skin. A new skin has already been grown underneath the old skin. Some snakes can live to be 40 years old.

Most snakes lay between three and sixteen eggs at a time.

hatch   come out of an egg.
shed   to take off. A snake's old skin peels off in one go.

Lazy snakes

Snakes spend much of the day lying around. If they are cold, they lie in the sun to warm up. If they get too hot, they crawl to a cooler place. Many snakes lie in wait for their prey. They have to keep very still, so that their prey doesn't see them.

Some snakes hang in sunny tree branches to warm up.

Hunting for food

Snakes spend some of their time looking for food. They are very good at hunting other animals. When they find a prey animal, some snakes eat it alive. Other snakes kill their prey by squeezing it with their bodies. Some snakes kill their prey with venom when they bite it with their deadly **fangs**.

This snake wraps around its prey and squeezes really hard to kill it.

fangs very sharp and long teeth. Snakes' fangs are hollow, like a straw. Venom flows through the fangs and into the prey.

Snakes and people

Some people keep snakes as pets. They need a special tank and food to keep them healthy.

Lots of people like to look at snakes in zoos. It is fun to watch these scaly animals bend and move!

Some small snakes that do not bite can make good pets.

A snake story

Why don't snakes have legs? People from the **continent** of Africa tell a story about this. They say that there were some animals that lived on a farm. Someone stole all of the food. The animals put sticky tar on the ground to trap the thief. The next day they found an animal stuck to the tar. It was the snake! The animals pulled the snake out, but his legs stayed stuck in the tar. From then on, the snake had to crawl on his belly!

continent one of Earth's seven big pieces of land.

Useful information

Read More

EDGE: Ultimate 20: Deadly Snakes by Tracey Turner (Franklin Watts, 2013)

Really Weird Animals: Snakes and Lizards by Clare Hibbert (Franklin Watts, 2012)

Animal Attack: Killer Snakes by Alex Woolf (Franklin Watts, 2014)

If You Were A: Snake by Clare Hibbert (Franklin Watts, 2013)

Websites

http://www.enchantedlearning.com/painting/snakes.shtml
This site has lots of snake colouring pages.

http://www.kidsbiology.com/animals-for-children.php
Then scroll down the list and click on 'snakes' to bring up a list of lots of different species of snake. Click on the name of a snake to find out some interesting facts.

Every effort has been made by the Publishers to ensure that these websites are suitable for children, that they are of the highest educational value and that they contain no inappropriate or offensive material. However, because of the nature of the Internet, it is impossible to guarantee that the contents of these sites will not be altered. We strongly advise that Internet access is supervised by a responsible adult.

Index